AKKAD

BOOK 2

SCRIPT & ARTWORK
CLARKE

COLOURS
MATHIEU
BARTHÉLÉMY

Original title: Akkad
Original edition: © Editions du Lombard (Dargaud-Lombard s.a.) 2021 by Clarke
www.lelombard.com

Translator: Jerome Saincantin
Editor: Erica Olson Jeffrey
Lettering and text layout: Design Amorandi
Printed in Spain by EGEDSA
This edition first published in Great Britain in 2022 by
Cinebook Ltd
56 Beech Avenue
Canterbury, Kent
CT4 7TA
www.cinebook.com
A CIP catalogue record for this book
is available from the British Library
ISBN 978-1-80044-056-2

IS IT DONE? DID YOU GET RID OF THE BODY?
YES.
WE'RE ALMOST FINISHED HERE. WE'LL STILL NEED YOU TO CONNECT THE GENERATORS ...
ARE THEY IN PLACE?
YES, WE HID THEM AROUND THE BACK.
DID YOU CHECK ON THE TANKS?
YEAH.
THE MAIN ONE IS STILL ABOUT TWO-THIRDS FULL. SHOULD BE ENOUGH.
PERFECT.
SPENGLER AND I ARE GOING TO FINISH CONFIGURING THE ACCELERATOR ON THE MAIN SYSTEM ...
YOU TWO ERASE ALL TRACKS AND HIDE THE TRUCK AGAIN.
I ... I CAN'T UNDERSTAND WHAT WE'RE DOING ... WHAT WE'RE PUTTING TOGETHER ... IT'S SO UNBELIEVABLY COMPLEX ...
WHAT IS IT?
AND **WHY** ARE WE DOING IT? WE'RE NOT MACHINES ...
SHOULDN'T WE BE EATING? DRINKING? GETTING SOME REST?!
STOP ASKING QUESTIONS. WE HAVE SO MUCH TO DO ...
65

WHAT? WITH HER WHOLE TEAM?!

MY RELATIONSHIP WITH GENERAL GERASIMOV CAME IN HANDY, BUT IT HAS ITS LIMITS. IT WAS THAT ... SOFI PAVLENKO WHO INSISTED.
ANYWAY, I IMAGINE SHE'LL BE MORE EFFECTIVE THAT WAY THAN ALONE.

FINE. I HAD TO GO THROUGH YOU BECAUSE SHE'D NEVER HAVE AGREED OTHERWISE ...
YOU HAVE NO IDEA HOW PERSUASIVE THOSE KIDS ARE. I HAD TO PLACE THEM IN COMPLETE ISOLATION ... WHEN THEY ESCAPE — WHEN, NOT IF — SOFI WILL BE THE ONLY ONE WHO CAN FIND THEM AGAIN ...
... BECAUSE, ALTHOUGH TO A MUCH LESSER DEGREE, SHE'S LIKE THEM.

SHE WAS IN ONE OF YOUR PROGRAMS, WAS SHE? NOW I SEE. SHE MUST HATE YOUR GUTS ...

I DON'T CARE WHAT YOU THINK. WHAT WE'RE DOING HERE GOES BEYOND YOUR MORALS.

GOODBYE.

66

LOS ANGELES AIRPORT, 6:00 AM ...
WELCOME TO THE USA ...
WE'LL BE TAKING OFF AGAIN IMMEDIATELY, HEADING TO PHOENIX ...
OUR BASE IS ON THE BORDER WITH NEW MEXICO. YOU'LL FIND FOOD INSIDE THE AIR-CRAFT ...
67

ADAM?
IT'S A FOUR-HOUR FLIGHT TO OUR DESTINATION.
I IMAGINE YOU READ THE BRIEFING MATERIAL ON YOUR WAY OVER. ANY QUESTIONS?
IT'S ALMOST TIME. ANYTHING TO REPORT?
N ... NO. I ... DON'T THINK THEY MOVED ...
THINK?
I ... I SPACED OUT. TEDIOUS JOB ...
THOSE KIDS ... THEY'RE ... SUPER-INTELLIGENT, IS THAT IT? LIKE, WITH SUPERPOWERS?!
I KNOW ...
LET'S GO. TIME TO CLEAN THE FREAK HOUSE.
68

HEAVENS, NO! THIS ISN'T SOME SUPERHERO COMIC BOOK.
OK. STAY BEHIND JENNY, TASER READY.
RELAX. WE DO THIS TWICE A WEEK ... OK, READY. OPEN IT.
NO, IT'S MORE THEIR ... INTELLECTUAL AND COGNITIVE ABILITIES. THEY'VE DEVELOPED TO ... PHENOMENAL LEVELS.
YOU MUST HAVE ISOLATED THEM, THOUGH ... DID THEY ... CONTROL THE GUARDS?
HOW? TELEPATHY OR SOME-THING?
ROOM SERVICE. ALL FIVE OF YOU, FACE AGAINST THE WALL AND HANDS BEHIND YOUR HEADS ...
THAT'S IT.
NO, NOT TELEPATHY.
MANIPULATION ...
BODY LANGUAGE AND WORDS USED WITH NEAR-SURGICAL PRECISION ...
JUST AN EXTRAORDINARY LEVEL OF PERSUASION ...
THEY CAN CONVINCE ANYONE IN MERE MOMENTS.
TO THEM, OUR MINDS LOOK ... BINARY. MALLEABLE. IT MUST SEEM SO ... EASY.
69

THEY CAN ANTICIPATE ...
... ANALYSE ...
... DEDUCE ...
... EXTRA-POLATE ...
... BUT NOT LEVITATE OR SHOOT LASER BEAMS OUT OF THEIR EYES, SORRY.
TO BE HONEST, I WISH THEY COULD. THAT WOULD MEAN NONE OF THIS IS REAL ...
AND ... WHAT YOU DID TO THEM ... IT WAS TO WIN THE WAR, WAS IT?
TO FIND A SOLUTION?
YES.
EEEEEEE

STAY AGAINST THE WALL!
THEY'RE STILL KIDS, THOUGH. I'M AFRAID THEY'RE COMPLETELY DISORIENTED BY WHAT'S HAPPENING TO THEM ...
DON'T MOVE!
WE HAVE TO LOOK AFTER THEM ...
... BUT ALSO MAKE SURE WE GET WHAT WE NEED FROM THEM ...
TK' PSCHHHHT
WHERE THEY ARE NOW ... I DOUBT OUR PROBLEMS ARE OF ANY INTEREST TO THEM.
AAAAAA
WOO WOO WOO WOO WOO WOO WOO WOO
THEY'RE ... DISCONNECTED FROM REALITY ...
71

... THEY LIVE IN A WORLD OF PROBABILITIES, QUANTIFICATIONS, ANALYSES ...
WOO
WOO
WOO
WOO
WE TURNED THEM INTO COMPUTERS, BUT WE ALSO FED THEIR FEARS, THEIR NEUROSES ...
KLAK
WOO
AND WHERE EXACTLY DO I COME IN?!
YOU ... YOU WENT THROUGH THE SAME THING THEY'RE GOING THROUGH NOW — EVEN IF IT WAS AN ORDER OF MAGNITUDE MILDER ... WE NEED SOMEONE WHO CAN ... COMMUNICATE WITH THEM.
AN INTERFACE.
TO BRING THEM BACK ...
... REMIND THEM WHAT WE'RE EXPECTING FROM THEM.
72

WOO
WOO
WOO
WOO
WOO
WOO
WOO
WOO
WOO
WOO
WOO
WOO
WOO
FREEZE!!
DON'T MOVE!
WOO
WOO
HANDS IN THE AIR!
ON THE DOUBLE!
73

IT'S HAPPENED!!

WHAT? WHAT'S HAPPENED?
THEY'VE ESCAPED!!
EARLY THIS MORNING.
WHY DIDN'T YOU INFORM US EARLIER?
THEY SABOTAGED THE SERVERS. COMMUNI-CATIONS ARE OUT OVER THE ENTIRE BASE.
WE'VE ONLY JUST RESTARTED THE SYSTEM ...
74

THEIR ESCAPE CAUSED A FIRE, TOO.
SO-O-O ... YOU'RE NOT NEEDED HERE AFTER ALL, RIGHT?
A LOT OF SYSTEMS WERE KNOCKED OUT.
WE DON'T KNOW THAT YET. JUST WAIT ...

WHAT DOES **THAT** MEAN?

WE'RE REVIEWING THE SECURITY FOOTAGE TO TRY TO UNDERSTAND WHAT ON EARTH HAPPENED ...

ROLL IT AGAIN, FROM THE TOP.

IT WAS HOUSECLEANING DAY. THE INSTRUCTIONS ARE CLEAR: THEY'RE TO STAY ON THEIR KNEES, FACING THE WALL ...

... THEN EVERYTHING WENT SIDEWAYS — ALMOST COMICALLY SO ...
HOLD IT.

HUH?
DO AS SHE ASKS.
CAN YOU SHOW THEM BEFORE THE WOMAN AND THE GUARDS COME IN?
75

LOOK. A SPIDER DRAWN ON THE SHEETS ...
... A DRESSER MOVED SO THAT THE GUARD WOULD HAVE TO STAND DIRECTLY BEHIND THE CLEANING LADY ...
... AND, FINALLY, THE LAMP ON THE DRESSER — TO NUDGE HIS ARM AS HE FIRES ...
INCREDIBLE ...
YOU MEAN THAT ALL OF THAT WAS ... PRE-MEDITATED?
THAT'S RIGHT. PRO-BABILITIES.
THEY HAVE THE PROCESSING POWER OF ... DOZENS OF COMPUTERS.
THEY ESCAPED BY DRAWING ON THEIR BEDSHEETS?!
THEN GOT RID OF THE GUARDS IN THE WAREHOUSE WITH THE SODIUM BATTERIES THEY TOOK FROM THE COOLING TOWERS OF THE SERVER ROOM ...
... THUS CAUSING AN HOURS-LONG SHUTDOWN.
THE SODIUM EXPLODED ON CONTACT WITH THE WATER FROM THE SPRINKLERS ... BRILLIANT.
WE MUST FIND THEM ...
MAYBE YOUR TEAM DIDN'T COME FOR NOTHING AFTER ALL.
ENOUGH.
CUT THE CRAP.
76

WHAT DO YOU MEAN?
THAT'S THE REAL REASON, RIGHT THERE.
THAT'S WHY YOU MADE US COME HERE. YOU KNEW IT WOULD HAPPEN, KNEW THEY'D ESCAPE ...
... AND KNEW YOU'D NEED SOMEONE LIKE ME TO TRACK THEM DOWN.
MEETING ALL MY EXPECTATIONS. NO SURPRISE ...
... YOU WERE ALWAYS THE MOST PRO-MISING.
NO.
77

YOU NEED US TO FIND YOUR TEENS? FINE.

SHOW US.

ALL CONTACTS WITH THE STAFF WERE STRICTLY LIMITED ...
... BUT THEY STILL MANAGED TO 'TURN' SOMEONE ...
HERE ARE THE FOUR MEN WHO DISAPPEARED.

WHY DID THEY LEAVE?
WE DON'T KNOW. WE SUPPOSE THEY WERE MANIPULATED INTO PREPARING OUR TEST SUBJECTS' ESCAPE.
THEY MUST BE WAITING FOR THEM OUTSIDE.

WHY DID YOUR GUINEA PIGS ESCAPE, THOUGH?

BECAUSE ... NONE OF THIS MATTERS THE LEAST BIT TO THEM.

THIS IS WHAT I WANTED TO AVOID. WE HAD TO KEEP THEM WITH US, PREVENT THEM FROM GETTING LOST IN THEIR OWN MINDS.
HUH?

YOU CANNOT IMAGINE HOW MUCH PAIN THOSE KIDS ARE IN FROM WHAT'S HAPPENING TO THEM ... THEIR EMOTIONS ... THEIR INTELLECT, WHAT THEY'RE GOING THROUGH ... IT'S THEIR SANCTUARY.

GETTING THE MOST OUT OF THEIR PHENOMENAL ABILITIES WHILE STILL PREVENTING THEM FROM LOSING THEMSELVES ... WE SHOULD HAVE CONTINUED TREATING THEM LIKE THE CONFUSED ADOLESCENTS THEY ARE.

78

THEY STOLE A TRUCK. THAT MEANS WE CAN FIND THEM ... SATELLITE PICTURES, SECURITY CAMERAS ...
WE LOST EVERYTHING WHEN THE BASE SYSTEM SHUT DOWN. AS FOR SATELLITES ... THIS AREA IS PEPPERED WITH FROZEN ZONES, SO THE COVERAGE AVAILABLE IS PATCHY AT BEST ...
THEN, LET'S FOLLOW THE FOUR MEN'S TRUCK ...
THEY HEADED NORTH-EAST, THEN STOLE SOME EQUIPMENT FROM A MILITARY LAB SOUTH OF ALBUQUERQUE BEFORE VANISHING.
EQUIPMENT?
YES. WE TURNED THEM INTO JUNKIES.
JUNKIES?
EXHILARATING SENSATIONS ... GIDDINESS ... THEN, AS WITH ANY OTHER FIX, THE CRASH ...
THE CRASH?
THE EFFECTS OF THE INJECTION ARE WEARING OFF. CAN YOU IMAGINE? ... COMING DOWN FROM THE DIZZYING HEIGHTS THEY REACHED?
NOT TO MENTION WITHDRAWAL SYMPTOMS ...
OH, MAN.
YOU MURDERING ...! I'LL—
WHY DIDN'T SOFI GO THROUGH THAT?
EXO-CELLS. WHAT THEY WERE GIVEN HAD LITTLE IN COMMON WITH MY PREVIOUS PROGRAMMES. THEY'VE GONE MUCH FURTHER ...
... AND WILL FALL FROM SO MUCH HIGHER.
ST ... STOP.
79

WHAT ABOUT THAT EQUIPMENT? THE STUFF THEY STOLE, I MEAN.
HERE. YOU NOW HAVE ACCESS TO THE THREE SCIENTIFIC AND MILITARY SITES THEY HIT AND THE LIST OF MISSING EQUIPMENT.
ENOUGH TO BUILD A FULL LAB. THEY'LL BE TRYING TO MAKE THEMSELVES A NEW DOSE ...
LIKE ALL JUNKIES, THEY'RE BEYOND MUNDANE CONSIDERATIONS ... THEY JUST WANT THEIR NEXT FIX.
BUT ... YOU SAID YOU HAD ACCESS TO ... WHAT WAS IT? EXO-CELLS?
I KNOW. THE WHOLE EXERCISE RESTED ON THOSE. THE KIDS WILL HAVE TO ...
YES?
LET'S GO.
... FIND SOME MORE THEMSELVES.
THIS LIST ... THE EQUIPMENT ... IT—
KLAK
80

NO! NOT THEM!
WHAT?
EVERYBODY OUT!
NOW!
WE'RE UNDER ATTACK!!

SOFI!!

FIND KARINA AND IVAN! WE NEED OUR WEAPONS!

OK. AGAINST THE TRUCK. AND KEEP YOUR HANDS WHERE I CAN SEE THEM ...

THEY'RE EVERY-WHERE!!

HOW DID WE NOT DETECT THEIR ARRIVAL?!
KARINA! GO HELP THE AMERICAN SOLDIERS! WE NEED TO EVACUATE!
NO!
YOU AND EVGENIY, GET TO THE CHOPPER AND FIND THEM!! KOLYA WILL COVER YOU!
I'M ON IT!
WHAT? BUT—
SHE'S RIGHT. WE HAVE TO FIND THE KIDS! LET'S GO!
YOU'RE COMING WITH US.
83

I'LL GET US OFF THE GROUND. GET IN!
WHAT ABOUT KOLYA?
NO TIME! IN!
KLAP
YOU CAN FLY THIS AIRCRAFT ?!
EVGENIY USED TO BE AN AIRBORNE FORCES PILOT!!
WE'RE ALL RATED ON AMERICAN EQUIPMENT ...
84

OK, GIVE ME A SECOND TO GET STABLE AND THEN TELL ME WHERE WE SHOULD BE HEADING.
EAST. THE LABS THEY STOLE FROM ... THEY'LL KEEP GOING IN THAT DIRECTION.
IT'S THE MOST RATIONAL CHOICE.
CAN YOU LOG ON TO THE MILITARY NETWORK?
FROM HERE? I THINK SO ...
LOCATE ALL ENEMY INCURSIONS IN THE SECTOR WE'RE HEADING INTO ...
IF THE KIDS NEED EXO-CELLS, THEY MUST HAVE FOUND A WAY TO ATTRACT THE INVADERS.
WHAT IS IT?
NOTHING.
OVER THERE. LOOK.
I KNOW. DON'T WORRY ...
85

I'M GOING TO NEED—
OH ...

... CRAP!!

BREAK! BREAK!!
WHAT DO YOU THINK I'M DOING?!
86

THAT WAS FREAKING CLOSE!
YOU WERE RIGHT, THOUGH. THAT MEANS WE'RE HEADING IN THE RIGHT DIRECTION.
THE PROBLEM IS THAT THE PRESENCE OF INVADERS PREVENTS COMMUNICATION WITH THE SATELLITES. I'LL HAVE NO WAY TO KNOW HOW MANY MIGHT BE IN THE AREA ...
WHAT ABOUT RADIO?
THAT'S NOT AFFECTED, OF COURSE.
GOOD. IN THAT CASE, CONTACT LOCAL POLICE FORCES ...
COLLATE ALL DATA RELATING TO GAS STATIONS BETWEEN CHIHUAHUA AND MESCALERO.
HUH?!
WHAT ARE YOU TALKING ABOUT?
87

THE EQUIPMENT THEY STOLE ... THEY'RE NOT BUILDING A STANDARD LAB. THEY STOLE ELECTROSTATIC COMPONENTS, NIOBIUM-TITANIUM CABLES, QUICK ACTIVATION PROCESSORS ...
WHATEVER THEY'RE BUILDING IS GOING TO NEED POWER. A LOT OF IT.
A POWER PLANT ...?
NO. YOURS ARE LIKE OURS — WATCHED BY THE MILITARY ...
THE CONSUMPTION SPIKE COULD BE DETECTED.
GASOLINE GENERATORS?
CENTRAL FUEL DEPOTS ARE UNDER MILITARY CONTROL TOO, BECAUSE OF THE SHORTAGES.
SO, A PRIVATE SOURCE — LIKE A GAS STATION.
IT HAS TO BE ISOLATED, MAYBE EVEN ABANDONED ...
SO, LOOK FOR ANYTHING UNUSUAL. IT'S OUR ONLY CHANCE.
WHY ALONG THAT STRETCH OF ROAD, EXACTLY?
THE ORDER IN WHICH THE LABS WERE ROBBED. THEY'RE HEADING SOUTH-EAST.
WHICH IS PREDICTABLE ... THE AREA IS DESERTED.
88

WHILE LOOKING FOR POLICE FREQUENCIES, I FOUND SOMETHING PECULIAR ...
WHAT IS IT?
THEY LOOK LIKE ... TRIANGULATION SIGNALS ...
PRETTY VAGUE, THOUGH.
WHO'S TRANS-MITTING?
I DON'T KNOW. THE STRANGEST PART IS THAT THEY POINT IN THE DIRECTION WE'RE HEADING ...
I DON'T UNDERSTAND ...
BASIC RADIOGONIOMETRY. BEACONS THAT EMIT RADIO SIGNALS. BY TRIANGULATING WITH SEVERAL OF THEM, YOU CAN PINPOINT A SPECIFIC LOCATION.
IN OTHER WORDS, SOMEONE IS BROADCASTING THE COORDINATES OF THE PLACE WE'RE LOOKING FOR ...
THERE ARE ONLY TWO SIGNALS ...
NOT ENOUGH.
INDEED. YOU NEED THREE FOR IT TO WORK — HENCE, 'TRIANGULATION'.
THE TWO BEACONS CAME ONLINE 30 MINUTES APART.
WHOEVER'S SENDING THAT LOCATION WANTS TO MAINTAIN THE SUSPENSE.
COULD IT HAVE ANYTHING TO DO WITH THE ALIENS POPPING UP IN OUR PATH?!
OF COURSE! THAT'S IT! IT'S THE KIDS — THEY'RE ATTRACTING THE SCARABS TOWARD THEIR DESTINATION! WE KNOW THEY'D NEED EXO-CELLS!
HOW FAR ARE WE FROM THE STATION?
EXACTLY 18 MINUTES. YOU CAN START THE THIRD SIGNAL ...
OK. DOWN TO THE SECOND.
HAHA!

IT'S SIMPLE. THEY'RE LURING THE SCARABS INTO A TRAP THEY'VE LAID SOMEWHERE WHERE THEY CAN CAPTURE THEM.
FOCUS ON WATCHING OUT FOR THAT THIRD BEACON.
NO! GO BACK TO POLICE FREQUENCIES! I WANT TO KNOW IF ANYTHING UNUSUAL HAPPENED!
WHAT'S WITH YOU?
I JUST DON'T BELIEVE THIS TRAP THEORY.
THOSE KIDS ... THEY'RE LIKE ... LIKE SURVEYORS OF THE FUTURE ...
THEY PREDICT EVERYTHING ...
NO, THOSE ALIENS ARE GOING TO COME IN HANDY FOR THEM SOMEWHERE DOWN THE LINE ...
THERE'S JUST NO WAY TO KNOW HOW, FOR NOW.
THEN, LET'S WAIT UNTIL WE'RE AT THE LINE ...
ANYTHING FROM THE POLICE YET?
BBC

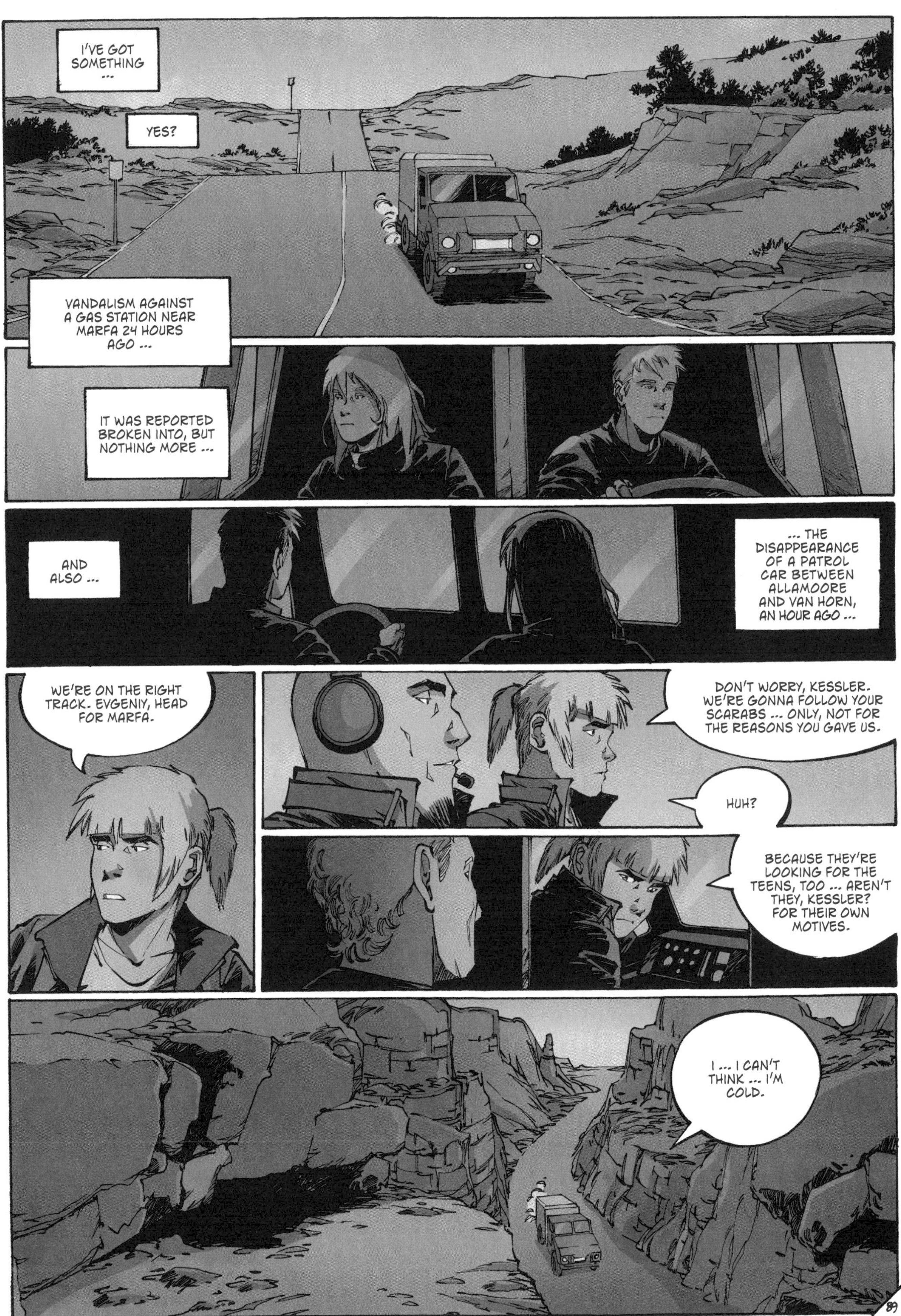
I'VE GOT SOMETHING ...
YES?
VANDALISM AGAINST A GAS STATION NEAR MARFA 24 HOURS AGO ...
IT WAS REPORTED BROKEN INTO, BUT NOTHING MORE ...
AND ALSO ...
... THE DISAPPEARANCE OF A PATROL CAR BETWEEN ALLAMOORE AND VAN HORN, AN HOUR AGO ...
WE'RE ON THE RIGHT TRACK. EVGENIY, HEAD FOR MARFA.
DON'T WORRY, KESSLER. WE'RE GONNA FOLLOW YOUR SCARABS ... ONLY, NOT FOR THE REASONS YOU GAVE US.
HUH?
BECAUSE THEY'RE LOOKING FOR THE TEENS, TOO ... AREN'T THEY, KESSLER? FOR THEIR OWN MOTIVES.
I ... I CAN'T THINK ... I'M COLD.

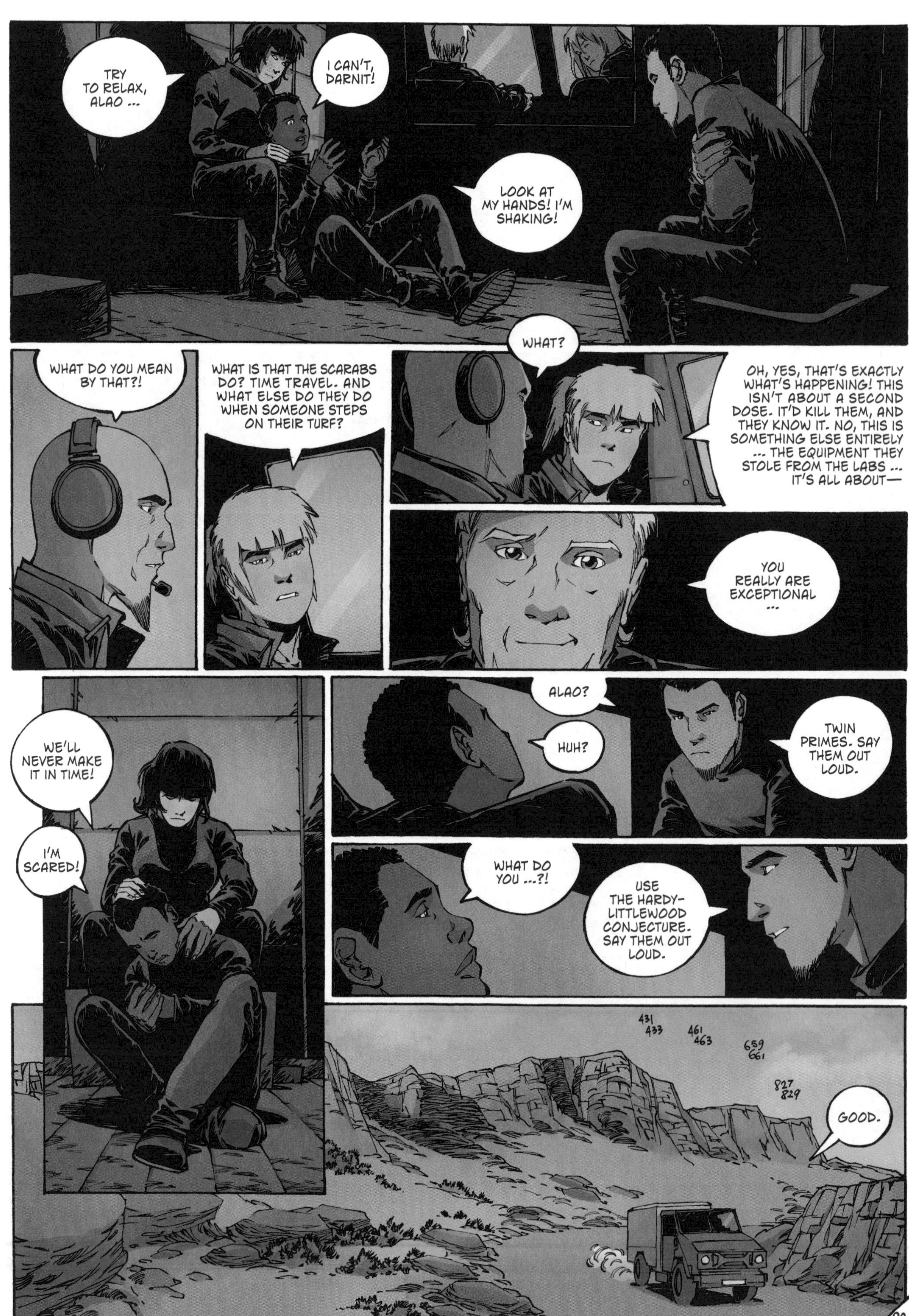
TRY TO RELAX, ALAO ...
I CAN'T, DARNIT!
LOOK AT MY HANDS! I'M SHAKING!
WHAT DO YOU MEAN BY THAT?!
WHAT IS THAT THE SCARABS DO? TIME TRAVEL. AND WHAT ELSE DO THEY DO WHEN SOMEONE STEPS ON THEIR TURF?
WHAT?
OH, YES, THAT'S EXACTLY WHAT'S HAPPENING! THIS ISN'T ABOUT A SECOND DOSE. IT'D KILL THEM, AND THEY KNOW IT. NO, THIS IS SOMETHING ELSE ENTIRELY ... THE EQUIPMENT THEY STOLE FROM THE LABS ... IT'S ALL ABOUT—
YOU REALLY ARE EXCEPTIONAL ...
WE'LL NEVER MAKE IT IN TIME!
I'M SCARED!
ALAO?
HUH?
TWIN PRIMES. SAY THEM OUT LOUD.
WHAT DO YOU ...?!
USE THE HARDY-LITTLEWOOD CONJECTURE. SAY THEM OUT LOUD.
431
433
461
463
659
661
827
829
GOOD.
90

WHAT?

WE ARE GOING TO FIND THEM. THANKS TO YOU.

HE FELL ASLEEP.
WE'RE ALMOST THERE ...

YOU KNEW!!
AND **YOU** TOOK ADVANTAGE OF THE FACT THAT I CAN'T LET GO OF THE CONTROLS!

YOU TURNED THOSE KIDS INTO GENIUSES WITH ONE GOAL IN MIND — AND ONLY ONE!!

THEY'LL CATCH UP TO US ...
OF COURSE.

THEY'RE USING A BELL V-280 ... WITH A CRUISING SPEED OF 320 MILES PER HOUR, THEY'LL CATCH US RIGHT IN FRONT OF THE STATION.
SCREW YOU ...
... I KNOW ALL THAT.
SOFI, WHAT IS IT? WHAT ARE THEY DOING?
THEY'RE BUILDING THEMSELVES A TIME MACHINE.
SO THEY CAN GET THE SAME FIX AGAIN.
AND AGAIN. AND AGAIN.
AND, IN DOING THAT, THEY'RE UNWITTINGLY GIVING US THE KEY TO WIN THIS WAR ...
I'M NOT OK ...
DIANE ...
I'M FORGETTING FIBONACCI'S SEQUENCE ...
... AND REMEMBERING THE BABY I LOST.
WITH WHAT THEY'VE INVENTED, WE CAN TRAVEL AS THE SCARABS DO — THROUGH TIME ... FIGHT THEM ON THEIR OWN TURF ...
... AND, YES, WIN THIS WAR.
92

THOSE JUNKIES HAD NO OTHER CHOICE IF THEY WANTED TO GET ANOTHER MAGIC FIX!!
YOU MANIPULATED THEM!!
YOU PUT THEIR BACKS AGAINST THE WALL AND DESTROYED THEIR LIVES!
I DON'T KNOW WHO'S THE WORSE MONSTER — THE INVADERS WE FIGHT OR YOU ...
WE'RE NEARING OUR DESTINATION ...
WHAT ABOUT THE MEN WE SENT TO BUILD THE MACHINE?
TOOLS ...
THAT'S NOT WHAT I MEANT.
I KNOW WHAT YOU MEANT.
BY NOW, THEY MUST BE LYING UNCONSCIOUS SOMEWHERE IN THE STATION, EXHAUSTED AND DEHYDRATED. THEY KEPT WORKING, NEVER STOPPING, NEVER UNDERSTANDING ...
93

SOFI, THE KIDS ... THEY DON'T GIVE A HOOT ABOUT OUR WAR, IS THAT IT?
INDEED. ALL THEY WANT IS TO GET HIGH ON PURE INTELLECT AGAIN.

BECAUSE OF WHAT YOU DID TO THEM!!
WHEN YOU REACH THAT LEVEL OF INTELLIGENCE, YOU CEASE TO SHOW ANY EMPATHY. THIS WAS THE ONLY—

ДЕРЬМО!* WHERE DID THAT ONE COME FROM?!
94

*CRAP!

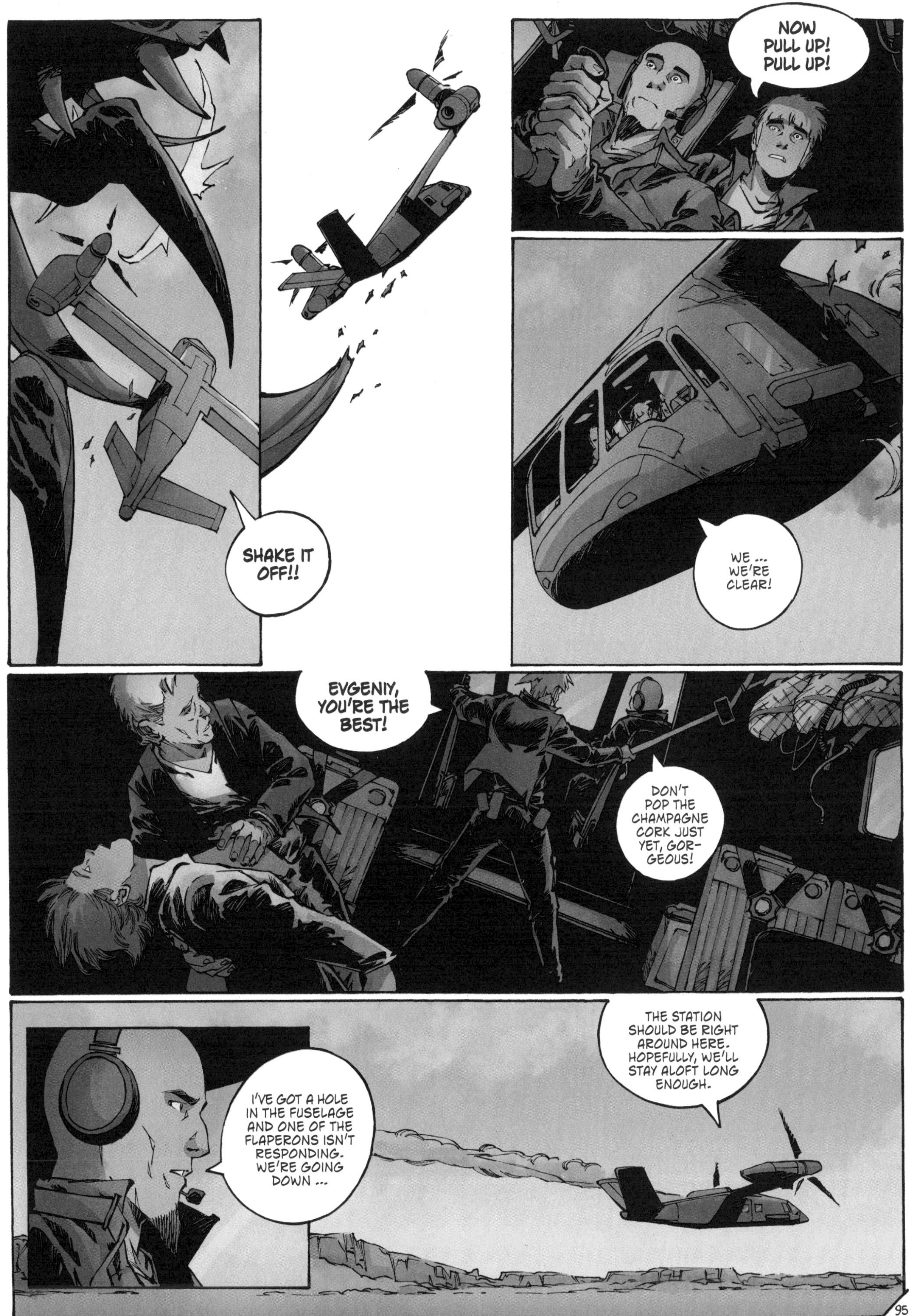
NOW PULL UP! PULL UP!
SHAKE IT OFF!!
WE ... WE'RE CLEAR!
EVGENIY, YOU'RE THE BEST!
DON'T POP THE CHAMPAGNE CORK JUST YET, GOR-GEOUS!
THE STATION SHOULD BE RIGHT AROUND HERE. HOPEFULLY, WE'LL STAY ALOFT LONG ENOUGH.
I'VE GOT A HOLE IN THE FUSELAGE AND ONE OF THE FLAPERONS ISN'T RESPONDING. WE'RE GOING DOWN ...
95

THOSE YOUNG PEOPLE WHO ... WHO ARE GOING TO GO BACK IN TIME ... WHEN DID YOU UNDERSTAND?
EARLY ON.
WE WERE MANIPULATED. I WAS BROUGHT HERE PURELY TO TRACK DOWN THOSE POOR KIDS.
WHY DID YOU HIDE THIS FROM US? YOUR PAST?
I DIDN'T HIDE ANYTHING. I MERELY TRIED TO FORGET.
I'M LIKE YOU. A SOLDIER. AND THAT'S ALL I WANT TO BE.
THERE.
THE STATION.
AND THE TRUCK! WE'VE ARRIVED AT THE SAME TIME ...
96

THE NACELLES WON'T ROTATE. THIS ISN'T GOING TO BE A PRETTY LANDING!

GOT IT. STRAPPING IN.

HANG ON TO SOMETHING, KESSLER. THIS'LL BE ROUGH.

CONTACT!

ALL RIGHT!
WE'RE STOPPING!!
97

BLAM
BLAM

K ... KESSLER? WHAT ...?

WH ... WHY?
98

THE PEOPLE WHO FUNDED THIS PROGRAMME HAVE NO INTENTION OF SHARING ITS RESULTS, I'M AFRAID ... TWO RUSSIAN SOLDIERS IN THE MIDDLE OF THIS ALL-AMERICAN LANDSCAPE, WELL ...
I'M SORRY.
EVGENIY ... NO ...

AS FAR AS I'M CONCERNED, THOSE KIDS CAN GO ROUND AND ROUND THEIR LITTLE TIME LOOP FOR ALL ETERNITY. IT DOESN'T MATTER.
WE HAVE THEIR MACHINE.

SPECIAL FORCES HAVE BEEN FOLLOWING OUR BEACON. THEY'LL BE HERE IN TWO MINUTES ...

IN THE MEANTIME, I'LL LET THE KIDS GET IN THERE, PRESS THE BUTTON, AND GO WHEREVER THEY WANT ...
NO ...

EVGENIY ... I DON'T WANT TO LOSE YOU ...

AND THERE'S THE CAVALRY!

?

YOU'RE NOT GONE YET? WHAT IS THIS — A LAST GOODBYE?
99

NOT GOODBYE, NO. NOT REALLY. RATHER THE OPPOSITE, IN FACT ...
WHAT? I DON'T UNDERSTAND.
HE DOESN'T UNDERSTAND.
I'M COLD. LET'S GO ...
WAIT. YOU KNOW I HAVE TO TELL HER. SHE NEEDS TO KNOW ...
SHE?
IF WE WANT TO RELIVE THE SAME EXPERIENCE, WE HAVE TO REMAIN IN THE SAME TIMELINE ...
WHAT DOES THAT MEAN?
I ... THINK OF THE WORLD AS A COMPUTER SYSTEM ...
NOW, IMAGINE THAT THIS ENVIRONMENT IS INFECTED WITH A VIRUS: TIME.
THE PASSAGE OF TIME.
IN THIS ANALOGY, WE'RE THE ANTIVIRUS. WE'RE AT THE HELM. AND WHEN EVERYTHING RESETS, WE KEEP GOING ...
YOU NEED TO REBOOT THE SYSTEM.
WHAT? WHAT ARE YOU TALKING ABOUT?!
IT MUST HAVE SEEMED OBVIOUS TO YOU: WE WOULD HAVE TO GO BACK IN TIME TO THE BEGINNING OF THE TREATMENT AND DO IT ALL AGAIN ...
YOU CREATED THIS PROGRAMME TO MAKE US CREATE WHAT YOU NEEDED.
A SINGLE INJECTION, IMPOSSIBLE TO RECREATE, AND ONE THAT GOT US INSTANTLY ADDICTED ...
SO, THAT'S WHAT WE DID — BUT WITH OUR OWN TWIST.
100

YOU'LL KEEP CIRCLING BACK TO THE BEGINNING, WHILE WE KEEP GOING ... AND TAKE OUR NEXT INJECTION.
IT'S THE WORLD AROUND US THAT WILL GO BACK, NOT US.
THAT'S WHAT THE MACHINE YOU WANTED TO GET YOUR HANDS ON REALLY DOES ...
... IT REBOOTS **YOUR** TIMELINE.
WHAT? NO ... **NO!!**
YOU'RE TELLING ME THAT **WE** ARE THE ONES IN A LOOP? FIGHTING THE WAR AGAINST THE SCARABS OVER AND OVER AGAIN?
HEY! NOW HE GETS IT.
FILTHY JUNKIES!
LET'S GO NOW ...
UNITS ONE AND TWO! ARE YOU ARMED?
ARE YOU ARMED?!
AFFIRMATIVE, SIR.
DESTROY THE GAS STATION!
RIGHT NOW!!
101

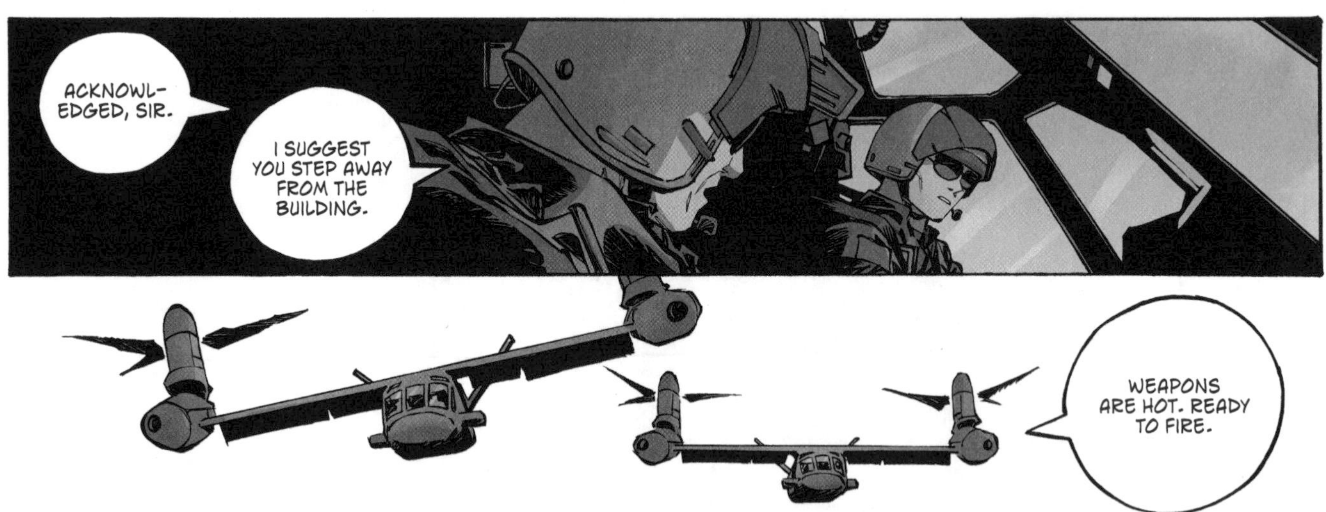
ACKNOWL-
EDGED, SIR.
I SUGGEST YOU STEP AWAY FROM THE BUILDING.
WEAPONS ARE HOT. READY TO FIRE.

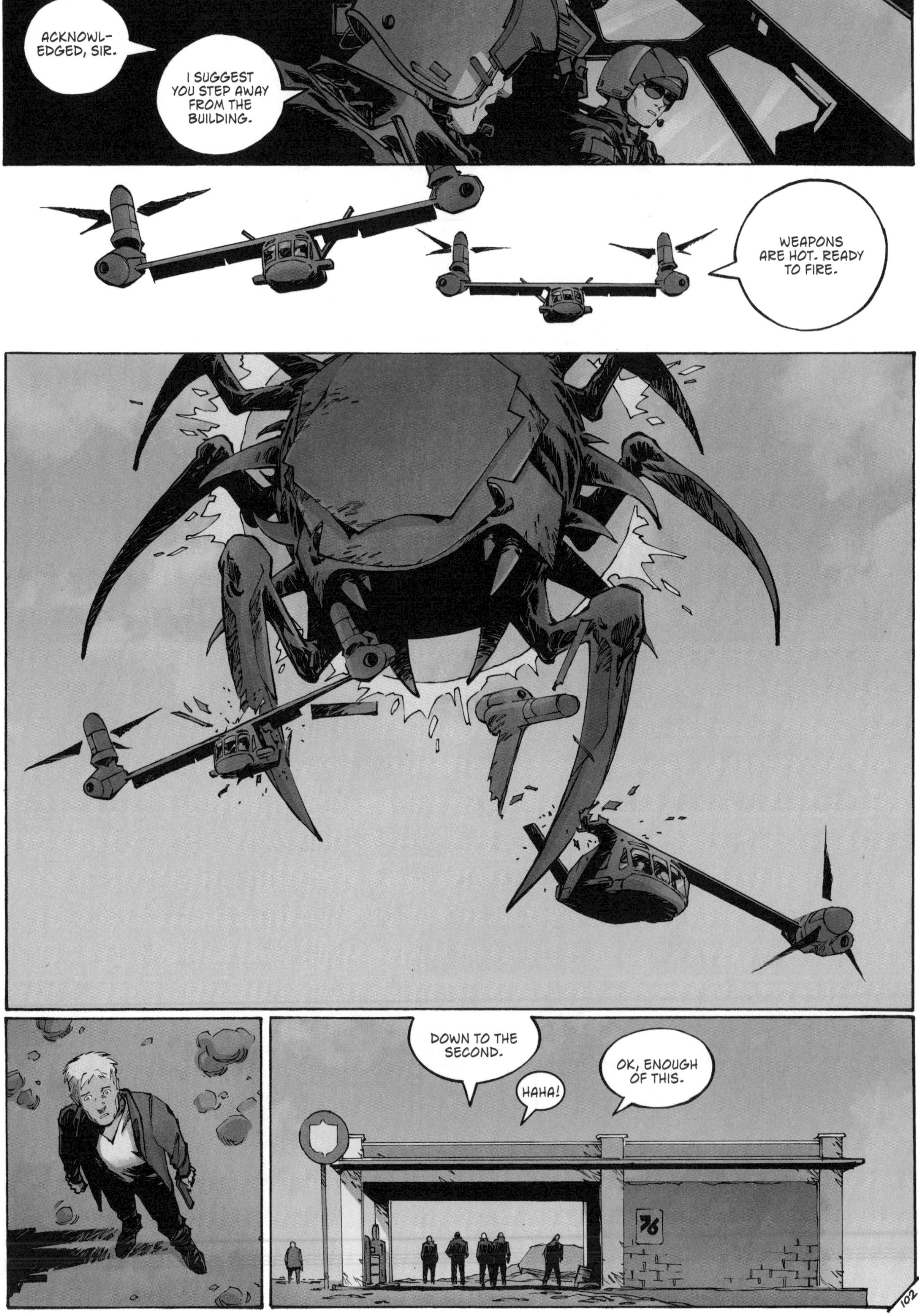

DOWN TO THE SECOND.
HAHA!
OK, ENOUGH OF THIS.
102

STOP THEM
... I CAN STILL
ST—
BLAM!
AAAH!
WHAT DID
YOU DO?!
WHAT DID
YOU DO?!
... AND
A BIT FOR ME,
AS WELL ...
I BROUGHT YOU
THE BILL AT LAST,
KESSLER, ON BEHALF
OF ALL YOUR GUINEA
PIGS ...
I GAVE
THOSE
CHILDREN
WHAT THEY
WANTED ...
NO ...
NO ...
103

I'LL SEE YOU REAL SOON, MY FRIEND ...

JUNE 2027.
KRASNOYARSK, RUSSIA.
ABANDONED KRASMAJ
NEIGHBOURHOOD.

SOFI!!!
SOFI!

YOU SCARED ME.
OK, THAT'S ENOUGH TRAINING FOR TODAY. WE'RE GOING BACK TO HQ.
NO, I'M FINE ... LET'S CONTINUE. I ...
THAT'S AN ORDER, LIEUTENANT ...
I ... YES, MAJOR.
GOOD.
DON'T TELL ME YOU WERE CONNECTED TO YOUR PAGE THE WHOLE TIME!
I SURE WAS! GOT IT ALL ON VID.
I TAKE GOOD CARE OF MY FANS.
COME ON.
WE HAVE A LONG DAY AHEAD OF US ...